D0510755

STEP-BY-STEP

MAKING PRINTS

DERI ROBINS

ILLUSTRATED BY JIM ROBINS

Kingfisher Books

Kingfisher Books,
Grisewood & Dempsey Ltd,
Elsley House,
24-30 Great Titchfield Street,
London W1P 7AD

First published in 1993 by
Kingfisher Books

10 9 8 7 6 5 4 3 2 1

© Grisewood & Dempsey Ltd
1993

All rights reserved. No part of this
publication may be reproduced,
stored in a retrieval system or
transmitted by any means,
electronic, mechanical,
photocopying or otherwise,
without the prior permission of
the publisher.

British Library Cataloguing in
Publication Data
A catalogue record for this book
is available from the British
Library.

ISBN 1 85697 1120

Designed by Ben White
Illustrations by Jim Robins
Photography by Rolf Cornell,
 SCL Photographic Services
Cover design by Terry Woodley
Typeset in 3B2 by
 Tracey McNerney

Printed in Hong Kong

CONTENTS

WHAT YOU NEED

Most of the prints shown in this book are made from ordinary bits and pieces from around the house. The only extra equipment you will need are brushes, a roller, plenty of paints and a good supply of paper!

Printers

Look around the home (and the garden) for objects to print with – anything that has an interesting shape or texture will do.

Keep a junk box, and save useful things such as old cardboard boxes, string, broken toys, offcuts of wood, corks, etc.

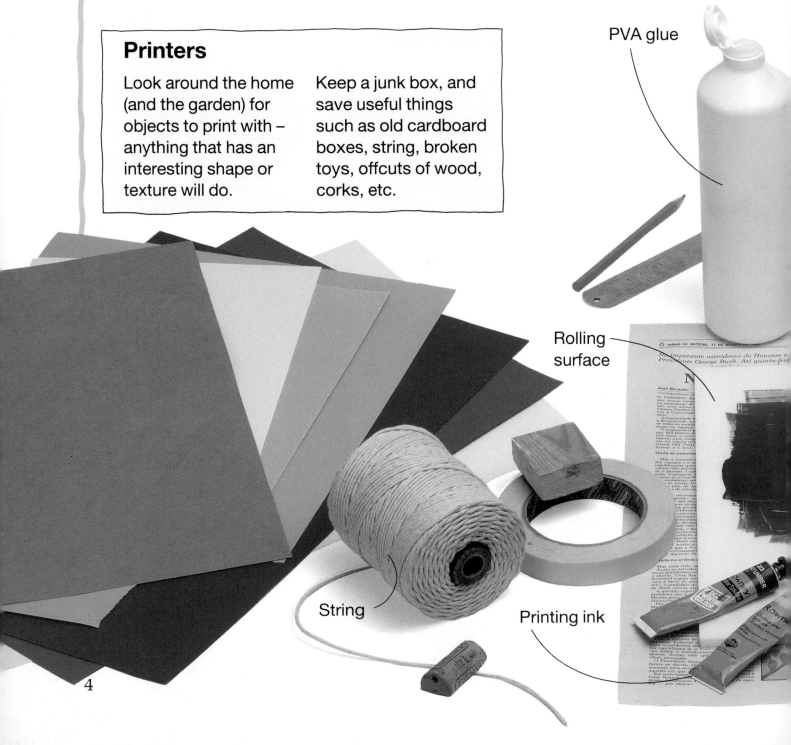

PVA glue

Rolling surface

String

Printing ink

Paints

Any thick paint can be used to make prints. Most of the prints in this book were made with printing inks – these can be bought from any art and craft shop. It's best to buy water-based inks, as these are the easiest and the cleanest to use. For marbling (see page 32) you will need some oil-based paint and white spirit. To print onto fabric and china (see page 34-37) you will need to buy special fabric and ceramic paints.

Tools of the Trade

For some of the prints in this book, you will need a roller and a large smooth surface such as a piece of formica.

For others, you will just need paint brushes and a saucer for mixing paints. You will also need some PVA glue, scissors and a craft knife. Finally, keep a supply of newspaper handy to protect your working area.

Pastry cutters

Fabric paint

Craft knife

Ceramic paint

Glitter

Roller

MAKING PRINTS

This book shows you how to carry out many simple printing methods, from relief printing and stencilling to marbling and monoprinting. Before you start, read the hints and tips on these pages carefully.

SAFETY NOTE

To carry out some of the activities in this book you will need to use a craft knife. These are very sharp, and can be dangerous unless used properly. Always make sure that an adult is around to help or supervise.

Printing Patterns

If you want to print a regular pattern, it's best to rule up your printing area before you begin. Use a pencil, and rub out the lines when the paint has dried out completely.

Applying Paint

Paint can be applied to a surface with either a brush or a roller – see which you find the easiest.

Rollers allow you to apply the paint quickly and evenly, but it can often be cheaper to squeeze out a small amount of paint and to apply it to your printer with a brush.

Mixing Prints

You can try overlapping different shapes and colours, as shown in the main picture. The flowers and leaves were cut from card (see page 16), and the grid design was made with a toy brick.

You can add the second layer when the first coat has dried, or when it is still wet – each method gives a different result. See which one you prefer.

Keep a sample of your most successful prints in a notebook or an album. You could also make a collage from various scraps of printed paper.

Experiment with paper – brown paper, newspaper and tissue all work well. You can also try using PVA instead of paint – sprinkle with glitter while it's still wet.

BODY PRINTS

In relief printing, an object is covered with paint or ink and then pressed down onto paper. The simplest relief prints of all are those done with your fingers – or your thumbs, toes or even your lips! Because body prints are so quick and easy, they make an ideal introduction to printing.

1

Mix up your paint with a little water in a saucer. It should be thick and sticky, not runny.

2

Roll the balls of your fingers from side to side in the ink. Press down onto the paper.

3

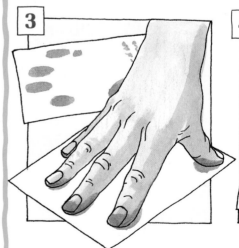

Take a print of the fingers and thumbs of both your hands, to make a complete fingerprint record.

4

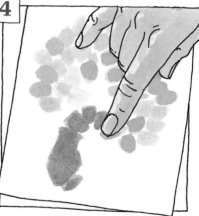

Try building pictures from finger-and-thumb prints. Use the sides as well as the balls of your fingers.

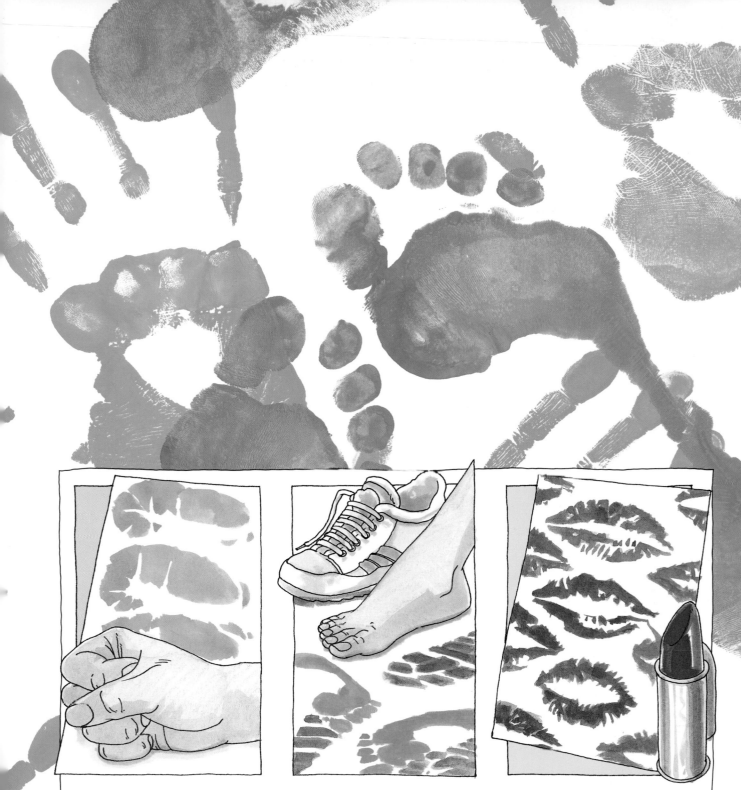

Roll out some paint on a large smooth surface. Take prints from your palm, fist, and the sides of your hands.

Make footprints – with or without your shoes on! Try taking a family record, from the smallest to the largest foot.

Give your lips a thick coat of lipstick. Part your lips slightly, then press lovingly onto a sheet of paper...

PRINTS FROM JUNK

Take prints from broken toys, bits of string, old keys, offcuts of wood – practically anything looks interesting if you repeat it often enough to make a pattern! Use junk to make relief prints, or try spattering with paint as shown opposite.

Below: These prints were made with the following (left to right): a piece of bubble-wrap; bits of old toys; a building block; half a cork.

Relief Prints

Use a brush to cover one side of your printer with paint. Press down onto paper, and repeat to build up a pattern. The pattern can be random, or even and regular as shown here.

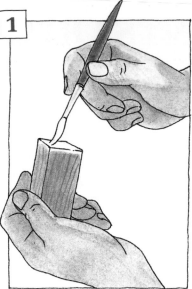

Spattering

Lay bits of junk on a sheet of paper. Dip an old toothbrush into paint, and run your finger over the brush in order to spatter the paint towards the paper.

Move all of the objects slightly, and spatter with a second colour.

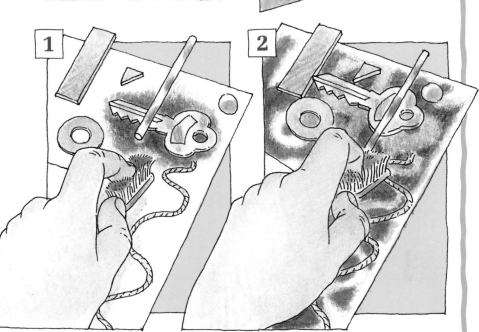

Mystery Print

Dip a piece of string into paint. Lay it onto a piece of paper, and put another piece of paper on top. Press down, and pull the string out. Take off the top paper to reveal your mystery print!

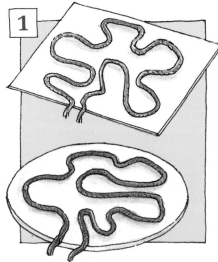

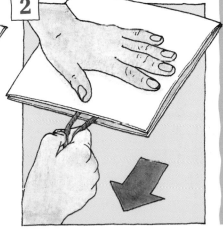

PRINTS OUTDOORS

When you've run out of household junk to print from, go and
see what you can find in the garden! Leaves, twigs, bark and
ferns all make lovely natural shapes and patterns. Look out
also for interesting 'street furniture' such as old manhole
covers – these can be used for taking rubbings.

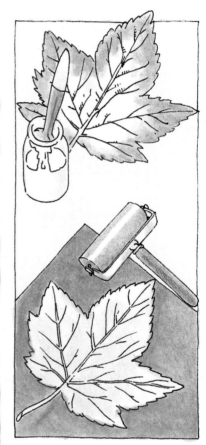

Leaf Prints

Using a brush or a
roller, apply thick paint
to the underside of a
leaf. Lay onto a piece
of paper, and press
down firmly.

Seashore Prints

Go beachcombing for
interesting things to
print with – try using
driftwood, dried sea-
weed, and shells of all
shapes and sizes.

Rubbings

Use wax crayons to
take rubbings from
manholes, or the bark
of a tree. Brush the
paper with thin paint –
what happens?

Use a few different leaves to build up a regular pattern. Try overlapping the first leaves with the second and third ones once the paint has dried.

PRINTS FROM FOOD

Potatoes are perfect for making pictures – try cutting them into different shapes to build up a lively frieze like the one shown below. Check the fruit and vegetable rack for other useful printers – you should be able to come up with a huge variety of fascinating shapes and textures.

Using Texture

Cut apples, carrots, cabbages and oranges into halves and segments. Dip them into a saucer of thick paint, and press down onto paper. Dried pasta and biscuits with raised surfaces also give good results.

Potato Prints

Cut a potato in half, and press a pastry cutter into one of the cut surfaces. Trim around the shape with a knife. Or make up your own shapes, and cut them out with the knife. Combine several shapes in one print, as below.

PRINTS FROM CARD

Save pieces of cardboard – empty tubes, boxes and packing material can all be used to make bright, colourful prints. Mix up some fairly thick paint, and spread evenly over a plate. Press the pieces of card into the paint, and print.

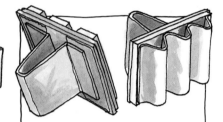 

Using Edges

Use tubes to print circles – dip the edges into thick paint, or apply with a brush. Try using straight edges to make lines, or bend them into shapes and tape together.

Textured Card

Cut shapes from corrugated card to make prints with a stripey texture. You could make simple handles by cutting strips of card, as shown, and gluing them to the backs.

Smooth Card

Cut pieces of thick, smooth card into stars, circles, strips, flowers and other shapes. To make the prints more interesting, cut out holes from the pieces of card.

Below: Card prints are perfect for making brightly-coloured wrapping paper – or, on a grander scale, for printing your own wallpaper!

Going Further

Cut two identical shapes from card – for example, a tiger or a zebra. Cut out extra details, such as the zebra's stripes, and glue these onto one of the pieces.

Roll thick paint over the plain piece of card, and press down to take a print. When this has dried, roll a darker colour over the raised surface on the second piece of card. Press this down over the first print.

17

LETTER PRESS

Cut big, bold letters and numbers from card – they're perfect for printing eye-catching posters, or your own personalized stationery. If you don't want to make a complete printing press, just cut out the letters or numbers you need.

1

Divide a thick piece of card into squares of equal size – about 2 x 2.5 cm. Make a square for each letter or number you want to print.

2

Draw the letters and numbers in the squares, making them thick and block-like. Cut them out carefully with a craft knife (ask an adult to help).

3

Cut another set of squares, the same size as the first. Stick the letters to the middle of the squares, using PVA. Glue them back to front, so that they will print the right way round.

4

Roll thick paint over the raised surface of the letters, and press down onto paper to print. If you are printing a whole word or sentence, it helps to draw rules in pencil first.

Name stamps

Instead of individual letter blocks, you may prefer to make a single block containing your name or initials.

Cut the letters you need from card in the usual way. Full stops can be made by using a hole puncher.

Cut a strip of card, as wide as the letters. Glue the letters in place, reading back to front.

PRINT A PICTURE

This cardboard printing press can be used to make your own special run of pictures or greetings cards. You will need to make a separate printing block for each colour you use.

1 Make a colour drawing. Cut a piece of tracing paper to fit the drawing, and trace the outlines with a soft pencil.

2 Cut four pieces of card, the same size as the tracing paper. Turn the tracing over and lay it over one piece of card.

3 Rub down all the outlines with a pencil, so that you have an exact copy of the drawing. Cut out all the shapes.

4 Tape the tracing to another piece of card. Choose one colour, and trace over all the objects in that colour.

5 Glue the shapes for that colour onto the outlines you have drawn on the card. Do the same for the other two colours.

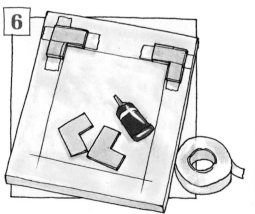

6 Make a base by drawing around one of the blocks onto a flat surface. Tape down corners cut from card.

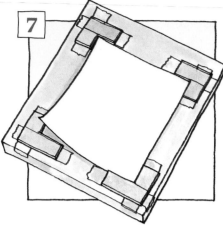

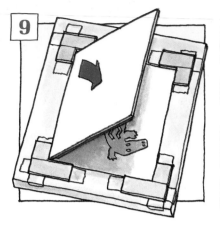

Cut some plain pieces of paper, the same size as the printing blocks. Lay one sheet of paper between the corners.

Mix up the paint so that it is ready to use. Take one of the printing blocks, and roll paint over the raised surface.

Using each of the colours in turn, press the printing blocks firmly down onto the same piece of paper.

MAKING BLOCKS

Long-lasting printing blocks can be made by gluing different objects to wood or thick card. Add colour and texture to your prints by using two or three blocks, as here. As well as string and foam, you could try using matchsticks, buttons, coins or dried spaghetti – the list is practically endless!

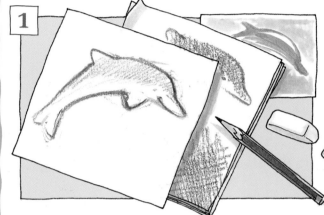

1 Make colour sketches for the design you want to print. Trace the outline onto some thin card, and cut out to make a template.

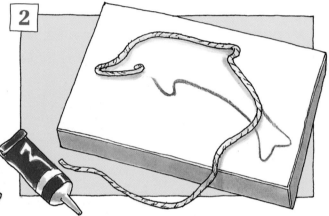

2 Turn the template the wrong way round, and draw around the outline onto an offcut of wood. Glue string to the outline.

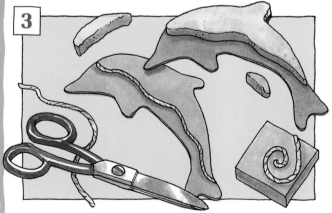

3 Cut two more templates from thick card. Glue string and foam to part of the surface, as shown. The fourth block is made from wood and string.

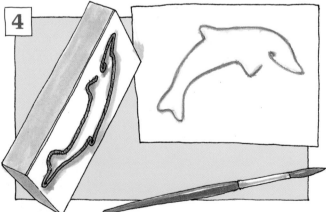

4 Roll paint over the blocks, and use them to make a number of prints. Add texture and colour by overprinting with the two card blocks.

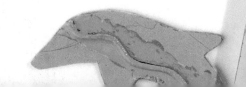

For a tiled effect, cut out your prints and glue them onto a large sheet of dark paper. Draw guidelines with a ruler and pencil first, to help you line the 'tiles' up. You could even use your design to print onto real bathroom tiles (see page 36).

SCRAPER PRINTS

The secret of scraper printing is to keep the paint very thick and even, and to make the pattern quickly before the paint has a chance to dry. Scrape lines and swirls with pieces of card – or draw a picture with the end of a paint brush.

1

Cut strips from thick card, each 10 cm long. Cut different-shaped notches from one side.

2

Roll a thick layer of paint or printing ink over a large, smooth surface.

3

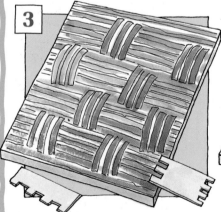

Use the strips of card to scrape lines in the paint – these lines can be short or long, straight, wavy or curved.

4

Lay a sheet of paper over the paint, and press firmly over the surface. Peel off the paper to see the print.

MONOPRINTS

A monoprint (literally, 'one print') cannot be repeated – each one you make will be unique. Like the scraper prints, you should take the print immediately, before the paint has had a chance to dry out.

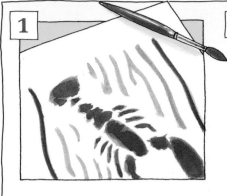

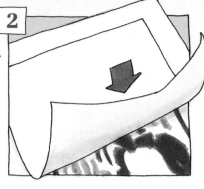

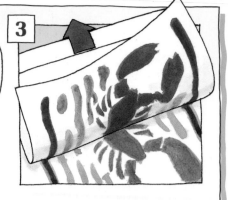

1 Paint a picture onto a flat piece of formica, marble or lino, using thick paint or printing ink. Keep the painting simple, and do it as quickly as possible.

2 Lay a clean piece of paper on top of the painting. Press down over the surface with your fingers, being careful not to smudge the paint underneath.

3 Peel the paper off the painted surface to see your print. The print should have a soft, slightly blurred texture, unlike a painting done with a brush.

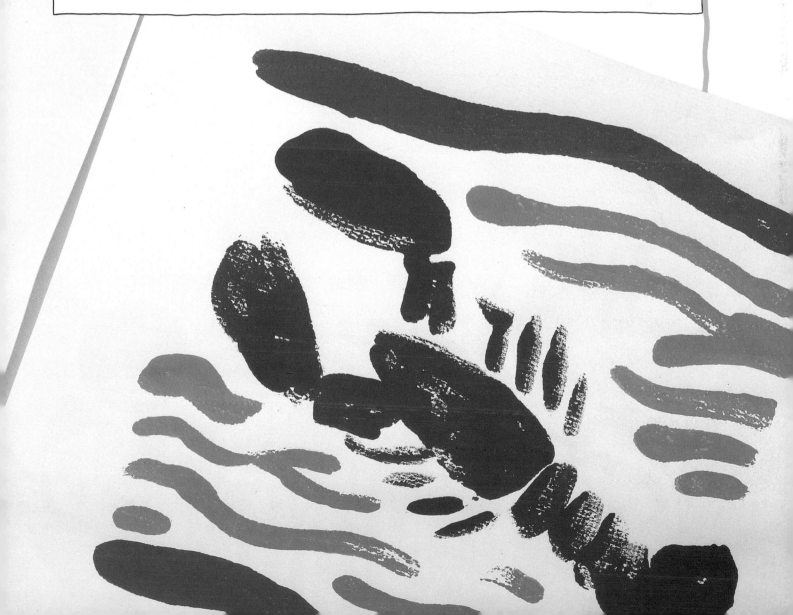

STENCILLING

The prints on these pages were all made with stencilling card, but any thin card would do. Ask an adult to help you cut out the shapes with a craft knife, and use a thick stencilling brush to stipple on the paint.

1
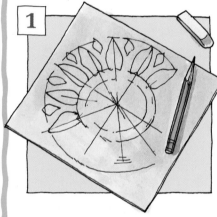

Draw a design onto the card with pencil. Try not to make the design too complicated.

2

Cut out with a craft knife (ask an adult to help). Leave 'bridges' between the holes.

3
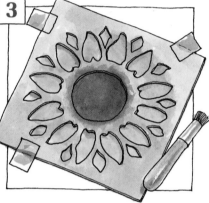

Tape the stencil to the paper, and stipple the paint through the holes with a stencil brush.

Doily Stencils

Make a doily by folding a square of paper in half several times. Snip holes from the folded edges, unfold the paper, and smooth out the creases.

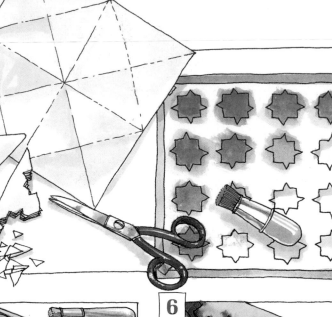

4

Before applying a second stencil, make sure that the paint from the first one has dried.

5

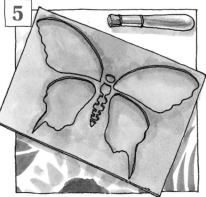

The butterfly was done in several stages. First, a stencil for the whole shape was used.

6

After the yellow paint had dried, two more stencils were used to print over the top.

 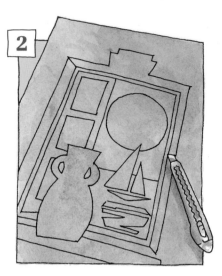 

Using Masks

Sketch out a design on a sheet of paper, using coloured pencils. Try to keep the design fairly simple, so that you can cut it out easily.

Trace your design onto stencilling card, and cut along the solid lines with a craft knife. Fit the pieces back together on a sheet of paper, rather like a jigsaw.

Tape down the outer frame. Choosing one colour at a time, take out all the pieces for that colour and spray the spaces left behind. When dry, replace the shapes and repeat for the next colour. Some areas (like the sea in our picture) could be sprayed with more than one colour.

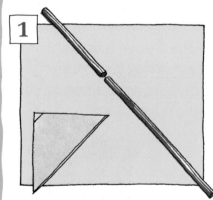 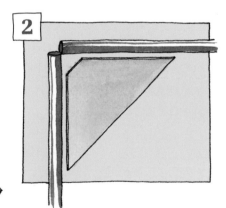

Make a Spray

Cut the top third off a thin plastic straw. Cut a triangle from card, and snip off the corner. Use this triangle to support the pieces of straw at a right angle, and use tape to hold all three parts in place.

Fill an egg cup with paint thinned with water. Dip the short end of the straw in the paint. Point the join at the paper, and blow gently down the other end.

Spraying paint is a messy business! Always surround your working area with lots of newspaper.

MARBLING

To make beautiful marbled papers, you will need some oil paints, white spirit and a large shallow tray or bowl filled with water. As water and oil don't mix, the oil paint will float on top of the water, and stick to the paper when you take a print.

1 Mix some oil paint with white spirit – the paint should be runny enough to fall in drips from the brush. Try using two different colours to start with.

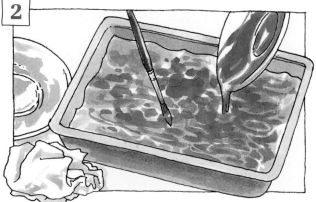

2 Use the brush to flick drops of paint over the water, or pour across the surface straight from the saucer. Swirl gently with the end of the brush.

3 Hold a sheet of paper by the opposite corners, and lay it gently over the surface. Smooth the surface to get rid of any air bubbles. The oil paint will cling to the paper.

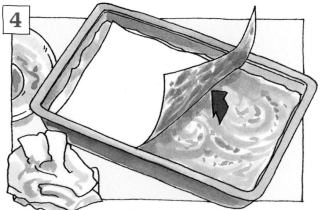

4 Lift off the paper and leave to dry. Add more paint to make a second print. Try adding wallpaper paste before adding paint – this helps you to swirl the paint into a feathery pattern.

In marbling, every print you take
will be different to the one before.
Experiment with two or more
colours, but be careful not
to mix them together so much
that the colours become muddy.

Try using your prints to cover a
notebook, or use them as special
wrapping paper.

FABRIC PRINTS

Fabric paints are sold in craft and hobby shops, and are just as easy to print with as ordinary paints and inks. Use them to print onto smooth materials – cotton is usually the best choice. Print onto T-shirts, sheets, pillowcases, socks or sneakers, or use scraps of material to make flags or banners.

1 Always wash and iron the fabric before you begin. If you're printing onto a T-shirt or a pillowcase, push a thick sheet of card between the two layers.

2 Pin the item to a flat piece of card, making sure that the surface is flat and smooth. Print in the normal way – for example, with a potato print as shown above.

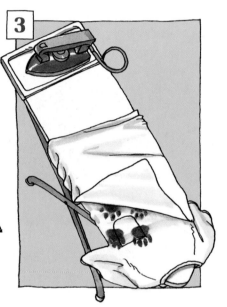

3 Most fabric paints need fixing with an iron – check the label, and ask an adult to help. Cover with a clean scrap of material, and iron over the top.

Right: The man-in-the-moon pillowcase was printed using masks (page 30). The spaces were stippled rather than sprayed, while the other pieces were held down by the fingers.

Above: Leaves were used to print the shirt (see page 12). The curtain was made from an old sheet stencilled with yellow stars (see page 28).

Left: The white T-shirt was decorated with a potato 'paw' print (page 15).

CHINA PRINTS

Transform boring pieces of china into collector's items with ceramic paints! We used the oil-based type which fixes as it dries. You can also buy water-based paints, which need to be fired in an oven. Both types are waterproof.

Curved surfaces need flexible printers. A square of sponge was glued to a small piece of wood to print a border onto a plate, mug and egg cup (shown in the photo).

The bathroom tiles were printed with shapes cut from card (see page 16). A simple square of card can easily be use to build up a harlequin pattern, using two colours.

The chicken design was stencilled, and the borders were printed with sponge. The design on the seashore plate (below), was made by stippling over masks cut from card.

Oil-based paints were used to print the china shown here. If you're using this type of paint, make sure you have plenty of white spirit to clean the brushes, and to wipe away any mistakes or spills.

37

USING PRINTS

Now that you know how to make prints, what are you going to do with them? Here are a few ideas.

Stationery

Print stationery for yourself or a friend – use plain writing paper, and make a set of matching envelopes.

Printing is also perfect for mass-producing greetings cards, gift tags and wrapping paper, and for taking the strain out of thank-you letters.

Decorating

Use prints to transform your room (furniture and floors will need a few coats of varnish to protect the paint). Try printing straight onto walls, or make a frieze from paper.

You can also try doors, picture frames, lampshades, curtains and duvet covers.

Parties

Paper tablecloths, cups, napkins and place settings can all be printed with (waterproof!) paints and inks.

To print glitter onto balloons, cut shapes from foam and dip into some PVA. Press onto the side of a blown-up balloon, and sprinkle with glitter.

Right: all the objects shown here have been decorated using printing methods from this book. To print onto furniture, use household emulsion or gloss paints.

MORE IDEAS

Finally, here are a few more printing suggestions you may like to try...

Rubber erasers make excellent printing blocks. Draw your design on one of the flat sides, and carefully cut around it with a craft knife. You should be left with a raised printing surface (see potato prints, page 15).

Sets of playing cards and dominoes can be turned out quickly using prints. You could also design your own fake banknotes...

Use your rubber blocks to print your own set of stamps! 'Sew' the perforations with an unthreaded sewing machine...

Letter magnets can be used to print strong, clear letters and numbers (see right).